DEMCO

Our Immune System

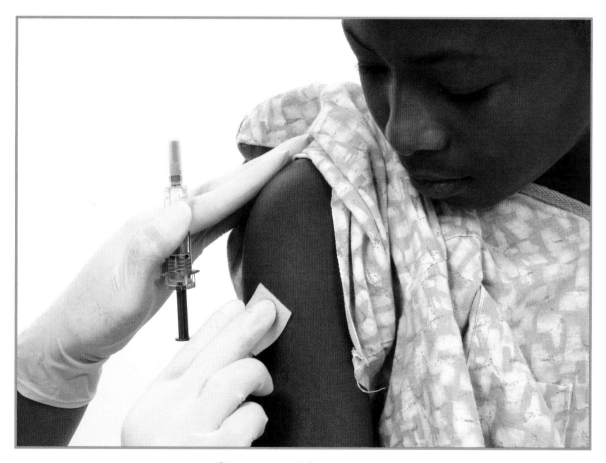

Susan Thames

Rourke
Publishing LLC
Vero Beach, Florida 32964

www.rourkepublishing.com

PHOTO CREDITS: © Jaimie Duplass: title page; © Renee Brady: pages 5, 9, 17, 22; © Robert Gubbins: page 11; © Greg Nicholas: page 13; © Sean Locke: page 19; © Franky De Meyer: page 21.

Editor: Robert Stengard-Olliges

Cover design by Michelle Moore.

J616.079
T

Library of Congress Cataloging-in-Publication Data

Thames, Susan.
  Our immune system / Susan Thames.
    p. cm. -- (Our bodies)
  Includes bibliographical references and index.
  ISBN 978-1-60044-511-8 (Hardcover)
  ISBN 978-1-60044-672-6 (Softcover)
  1. Immune system--Juvenile literature. I. Title.
  QR181.8.T34 2008
  616.07'9--dc22
                          2007011807

10/07
donation
22.79

Printed in the USA

CG/CG

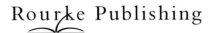

Rourke Publishing

www.rourkepublishing.com – rourke@rourkepublishing.com
Post Office Box 3328, Vero Beach, FL 32964

Table of Contents

Germs

Germs are everywhere.
Germs are too small to see.

Some germs can make you sick.

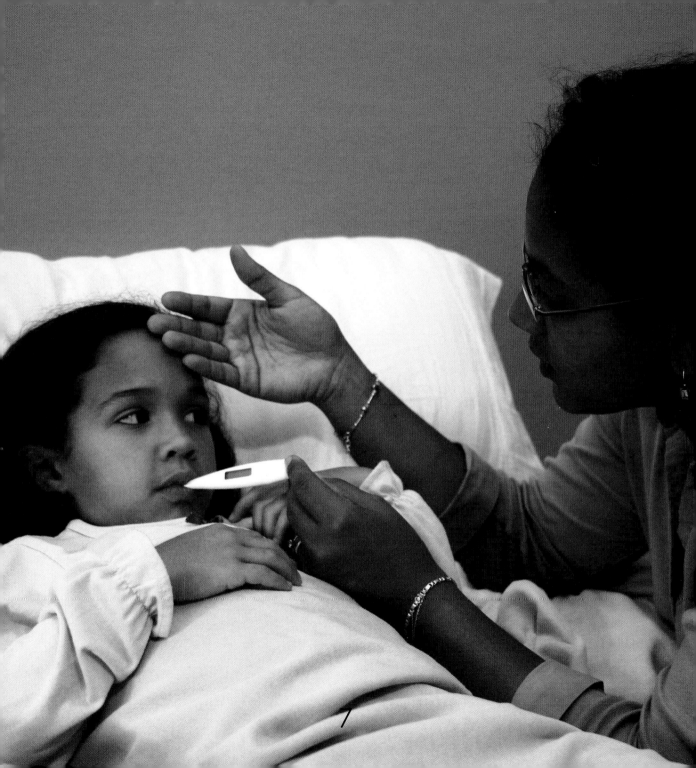

How can you spread germs?

Sneezing

How can you stop germs?

Washing Hands

Your Immune System

Your **immune system** protects your body.

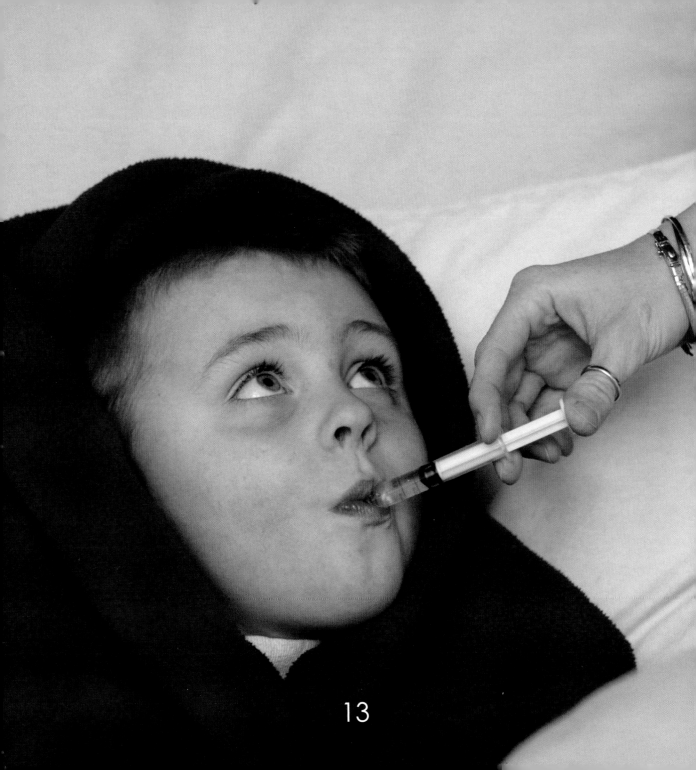

It helps your body fight germs.

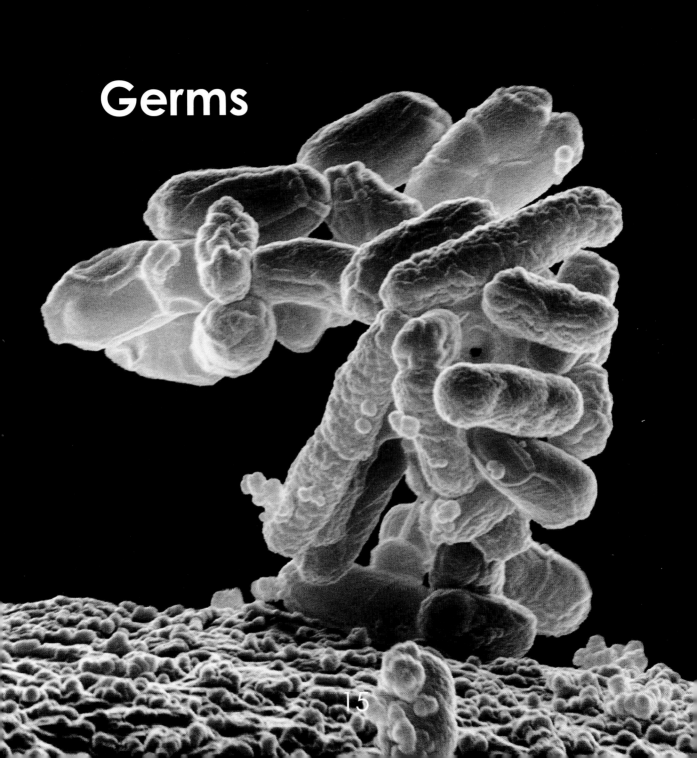

Germs

How can you fight germs?

Exercise

Doctors can give you medicine too.

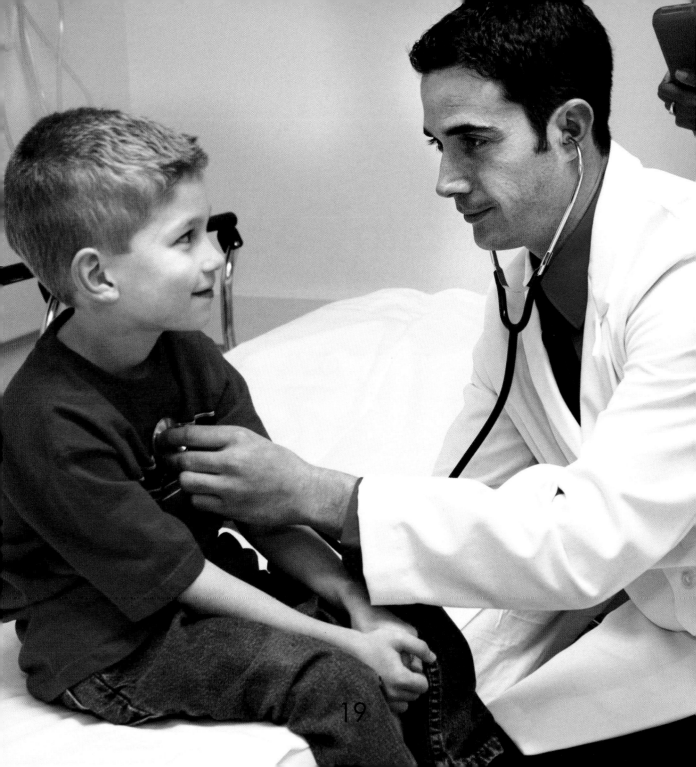

19

Healthy Body

Protect your body
from germs...

...because germs
are everywhere!

Glossary

exercise (EK sur size)— to move your body in a way that makes you strong and healthy

germs (JURMZ) — tiny living things that can make you sick

immune system (i MYOON SISS tuhm)— body system that protects you from germs

protect (pruh TEKT)— keep safe

Index

Further Reading

Mitchell, Melanie. *Killing Germs*. Lerner Publications, 2006.
Oetting, Judy. *Germs*. Scholastic, 2006.

Websites to Visit

www.kidshealth.org

www.healthfinder.gov/kids

www.yucky.discovery.com

About the Author

Susan Thames, a former elementary school teacher, lives in Tampa, Florida. She enjoys spending time with her grandsons and hopes to instill in them a love of reading and a passion for travel.